Principles

for

Po Promise

God's System of Seedtime and Harvest

Paula White

Principles for Possessing Your Promise:
God's System of Seedtime and Harvest

Copyright © 2004 Paula White

Published by Scribe
706 McCrory Creek Road
Nashville, TN 37214

Published in Partnership with Paula White Ministries
2511 Without Walls International Place
Tampa, FL 33607

Editorial and Project Management by Dan and Angela DePriest of Scribe, Nashville, Tennessee
Cover and Typesetting Design by Crosslin Creative of Thompson's Station, Tennessee
Printing by Edwards Brothers Incorporated of Ann Arbor, Michigan

All Scripture quotations in this book, unless otherwise indicated, are taken from the *Holy Bible King James Version.*

ISBN: 0-9760-0660-X

Printed in the United States of America
06 07 / CHG / 4 3 2

Table of Contents

Author's Preface

We live in extraordinary times. Not since the early days of the church has there been such manifest evidence of God's spirit moving in the world. And with it has come an increase in the enemy's rage and destructive activity. Recent years have seen miraculous transformations in hundreds of obscure areas of the world brought about by repentance and submission to the Lordship of Jesus. The Spirit of God is moving upon the earth and within His church to call His own out of bondage and poverty.

At the same time, Satan is inciting more and more hostility between nations and people groups. Divorce, pornography, and broken covenants of every kind have become epidemic—even in the church.

But we know Christ has already won this battle—Hallelujah! The bondage, war, and poverty that may be inescapable in an unrepentant world need not be found in the body of Christ. For all who are in Christ, there are promises of peace, promises of strength to overcome obstacles, promises of victory over all the works and deceit of the devil.

You have been called by God to triumph over bondage and to prosper.

In this book, I will teach you the source and meaning of this prosperity and how to walk in it. I will teach you how to take possession of the promise God has given you in His Word, as well as all the promises He has shown you for your individual life in Him.

I'll begin in Part I by helping you *position* yourself to receive God's promise and I'll show you the six Biblical reasons for lack in your life. Oh, yes! There are reasons!

Then, in Part II I'll teach you the principle of Firstfruits. Think of this principle as you would the foundation of a house. It defines the shape of the house and supports every part of it. It's the first thing you establish before building a life of taking possession of the promise.

After completing this foundation we will begin building the walls, rooms, and sturdy floors of a faith walk that wins the day everyday in Part III — God's system of seedtime and harvest. These building materials will be the principles of active faith and uncompromised trust in Jesus that result in taking possession of God's promise through the wisdom and action of sowing and reaping.

In Part IV of this book, we will take a practical approach to how you can change your perception of one specific area of your life—your finances. The keys to the kingdom apply to all things. There's no place it doesn't apply. But in this section, we'll look at how we apply these principles specifically in the area of your personal finances. We'll examine your perception of money and how the principles you've learned in this book can change how you use your money and bring your perception of wealth into alignment with God's perception of wealth.

You can prosper, brothers and sisters! The battle is already won. You need only to use the keys to the kingdom left to you by our victorious General. Unlock the door separating you from victory. Enter the world on the other side where nothing is impossible and even loss becomes multiplied gain. Enter the world where all things are possible to him who believeth (Mark 9:23).

Paula White
July 2004

Spirit of the Living God, anoint me to teach what thus saith the Lord but also anoint those who are touched by this teaching and who carry it into the work they do in Your name. Psalm 10:17 says, "thou hast heard the desire of the humble: thou wilt prepare their heart, thou wilt cause thine ear to hear." Living God, we ask for Your preparation now. Remove any blinders that would deceive us, hold us back, or hinder us. We stand in an awesome place with a spirit of expectation. We are ready to look to the horizon and receive what You have made for us. Position us by Your Word. Let Your principles grow deep within our hearts. Make our womb strong enough to deliver what thus saith the Lord. Amen.

Part I

Positioning Yourself to Receive God's Promise

"I am come that they might have life,
and that they might have it more abundantly."

(John 10:10)

A Position to Receive

How many of you believe this will be your best year ever? Do you believe this is your time of harvest? Your time of increase? Your time of abundance? If you believe these statements are true, let me tell you something that might shock you. You can go through this year saying, "I'm the head and not the tail" and still file bankruptcy. You can say, "My husband is the high priest of the household" and still watch him go down to the courthouse and file divorce papers.

You might believe God has promised you many things but you will never see them manifested in your life until you are properly positioned to receive them. You can plead promises all day long, pray until you're blue in the face, and fast until you're as skinny as my pinkie finger, but until you learn to position yourself to receive by living out God's principles, your pleading will be in vain. Why? Because God is a God of principles and you must live by His principles if you are to receive His promises. Until you are operating in these principles, God's promises for you won't come to pass. Pleading promises won't help you if you are breaking God's principles.

Remember, it's not only what you *say* that brings fulfillment of God's promises, it's your *position to receive*.

I want to help position you to receive the increase, the harvest, and the abundance God has for you. So, let's learn these principles. They are principles pregnant with the authority of the Word of God and will bring you into that place of promise.

God Wants You Blessed

Let's begin by establishing one thing: When God says He's going to bless you and prosper you, He's not just talking about money. The word *prosperity* is a wholeness word. It encompasses spirit, soul, body, mind, and emotions. Yes, it is inclusive of money—God wants your needs met and your desires fulfilled—but it's not *just* about money. God doesn't want you to have only financial peace and be broke, busted, and disgusted in every other area of your life. *Prosperity* means nothing is missing or broken—nothing is lacking.

We find Jesus' mission statement in John 10:10:

> *"I am come that they might have life,*
> *and that they might have it more abundantly."*

Jesus says His mission is to give you life to the absolute fullest. He was not just promising you heaven after you die. He wants you to believe in the abundant eternal life He bought for you and it begins where you are right now, fulfilling the will of God here on earth. He wants you to live life, enjoy life, and have life to the fullest.

So, we've established that God wants you blessed. Now let's move into this area of prosperity a little more. Proverbs 23:7 says, *"For as he thinketh in his heart, so is he."* If you can become prosperous in your soul, everything else in your life will follow—your health, your relationships, even your money.

Now, open your Bible to 3 John 2. It says:

"Beloved, I wish above all things that thou mayest prosper and be in health, even as thy soul prospereth."

The Hebrew word for *prosper* is "tsalach" which means "to push forward." Whenever you push forward, God will slap success on it. When you push forward for your business, God will slap success on it. When you push forward for your family, God will slap success on it. When you push forward to your dream, God will slap success on it.

Now notice the verse says, "AS thy soul prospereth" [emphasis mine]. You see, the Word is giving birth as it is being preached. God wants you to have a balanced life. He wants your business affairs, your family, your emotions, your ministry, and every part of your life to prosper to the same degree "AS thy soul prospereth." If your soul is depleted, there will be lack in all the other areas of your life. Your affairs in life should be a reflection of the condition of your soul.

Next, let's look at what Psalm 35:27 says:

"Let them shout for joy, and be glad, that favour my righteous cause: yea, let them say continually, Let the LORD be magnified, which hath pleasure in the prosperity of his servant."

Magnify is a Hebrew word that means "to swell up." Psalm 35:27 says to let God *swell up* who has pleasure in the prosperity of His servant. God actually *swells* with joy when you prosper! How does the Lord begin to prosper you? Psalm 115:14 says:

> *"The LORD shall increase you more and more, you and your children."*

God wants to increase you. He wants to expand and bless you. For those who fear the Lord and honor Him, He says He will cause you to increase more and more. God doesn't want you going backward. He doesn't want you to be immobile. He wants to move you into the promises He has made and increase you "more and more"!

The Word says Jesus went to prepare a place for us (John 14:2). The struggle is not in preparing the *place*—it's in preparing the *people*. You see, we are often hooked on surviving. We are hooked on waiting for miracles to occur. But miracles, signs, and wonders are for unbelievers. God doesn't want you surviving on miracles. He doesn't want you surviving on manna. He wants you to live in the abundance and overflow of His blessings. He doesn't want you to live in Egypt—the land of *not* enough; or the wilderness—the land of *just* enough. He wants you to live in Canaan—the land of *more* than enough.

Psalm 5:12 declares:

> *"For thou, LORD, wilt bless the righteous; with favour wilt thou compass him as with a shield."*

Yes! With favor He will surround you as a shield! The imagery here is breathtaking. Imagine your God wrapped around you like a shield, giving you protection and strength. You are a mighty fortress because of who you are in Him. And He will bless you because you are righteous through Him.

Remember, the word *bless* is not focused solely on money. It means "to empower, to prosper, to succeed." It means whatever you do, God will empower you to prosper and succeed. He wants to bless your marriage, your money, your ministry, your children, your mind, and your body. He wants to empower you to prosper and succeed.

Do you understand this concept of being righteous? You are righteous in God's eyes! But not because of yourself. You are righteous in God's eyes because of the blood of Christ Jesus. And because of your righteousness, God will give you favor. His favor will give you access to places you don't even deserve. He's going to cause people—even your enemies who rise up against you—to bless you. Even the people who don't like you, who talk bad about you, God will cause them to bless you.

Continue in the Word

John 8:31-32 says:

"Then said Jesus to those Jews which believed on him, If ye continue in my word, then are ye my disciples indeed; And ye shall know the truth, and the truth shall make you free."

When Jesus says to continue in His word, He doesn't mean for you to test or try out the Word. *Continue* means "to remain, to dwell, to abide, to endure, to stand firm under pressure." It doesn't mean you can test it out on Monday and become weary on Wednesday. The Word is like a mirror. When you look into it, it won't lie to you. You'll only see what's true. That means you stand firm no matter what you feel. You walk by faith, not by your feelings.

Hebrews 10:38 says, "the just shall live by faith." We shall live by the Word of God. Romans 10:17 tells us faith cometh by hearing and hearing by the Word of God. Don't live by what you *feel*. Live by what you *know*. That's faith.

So if you stay in the Word, then what? Then, according to John 8:31-32, you are His disciples and you shall know the truth and the truth shall make you free! Let that bake for a minute, will you? The *truth* you *know* shall make you *free*, it will *liberate* you, and it will bring you into the promises of God.

You see, what you don't know is killing you. The Word is your covenant. It is your legal, binding contract. The problem is a lot of people don't know they have this contract.

This reminds me of a homeless lady who died a beggar. She died on the streets with no roof over her head. She had no provision on her table. When she was buried, lawyers discovered she had inherited a great sum of money. Because she didn't know how to read, she never read the covenant in the document she held in her hands. She was a multi-millionaire and never knew it!

Many of us are like this woman. We are rich. We have inherited the promises of God. But we haven't read and acted on our covenant rights.

Some Christians may be uncomfortable with the word "rights" when it comes to the promises of God. But as we have already acknowledged, we didn't earn our places in the kingdom. We are *given* the power to become the sons of God (John 1:12).

When God gives you the treasures of the kingdom, it is not arrogant to say, "This is mine from the hand of God." In fact, it is worship. The thing given glorifies the giver. This is why God is swelled up (magnified) by blessing you. God is glorified when you can rejoice in the presence of others by saying, "Look what the Lord did for me! He did it for no other reason than to show His goodness."

Six Biblical Reasons for Lack in Your Life

We have established that God desires you to prosper, to be blessed, and to be increased. So, why is there lack in your life? The problem is not on the *giving* end, or *God's* end. Therefore, it must be on the *receiving* end, or *your* end. And lack is not just about being short of money. Lack can be experienced in many ways. Lack is a place of depletion, a place where fullness does not flow in your life.

You may lack joy, peace in your relationships or peace with yourself, wisdom, strength, or money. You may lack the power to overcome fear and doubt. You may lack the spiritual intimacy with Jesus that can daily restore your soul. You may lack the spiritual strength to guard your heart from the enemy's distractions. But I'm here to teach you the devil is a liar! Your Savior died on an old rugged cross and rose from the dead to give you life and life more abundantly!

You don't need strength to guard your heart from the devil's lies. You just need to know the truth in God's Word and then stand on it. Stand on it even if there are times when you don't feel like it. Faith is *acting* on what you know, not *feeling* or *understanding* what you know. Faith positions you to receive. Go on and tell the devil, "You are a liar! I'm going to find out my rights!"

So, let's identify and examine six things the Bible says can cause the spirit of lack in your life because when you close those doors, you can begin to position yourself in a place of harvest, abundance, and increase.

The Unteachable Spirit

The first cause of spiritual poverty is an unteachable spirit. There are many ways you can have an unteachable spirit. One way is by refusing instruction. Proverbs 13:18 says:

"Poverty and shame shall be to him that refuseth instruction: but he that regardeth reproof shall be honoured."

What's that you say? You think you know it all? Well, just shut this book, shut your Bible, shut your notebook, and put down your highlighter pen. Don't read another word—because no one can help you. Rebellion is a sin and sin separates you from God's abundance. People who think they know everything can't be taught anything. No one can speak into their lives and they have no accountability. No one can bring correction to them.

If you have an unteachable spirit, you will not move into the place God has for you because the Bible says an unteachable spirit brings poverty upon you. You can be in one Scripture for the rest of your life and never receive the depth God can unlock within it. There is so much wisdom and power God has for you! You shouldn't be the same person you were 10 years ago. If you are, something is wrong! You should be growing from glory to glory to glory! But you can't grow unless you can be taught.

Another, more devastating, way you can have an unteachable spirit is by refusing to forgive. The Bible says to forgive, not for *their* sake but for *your* sake. Forgiving releases you from bondage. Matthew 18:21 says we must forgive "Until seventy times seven." God knew we would need to do a lot of forgiving in a day!

How can you ever expect to be forgiven for the wrongs you've committed if you are not willing to forgive?

You can't even begin to understand the principle of Firstfruits unless you break free from unforgiveness. You can never see the power of God's system of seedtime and harvest while you hold an unforgiving heart. You can't position yourself to receive the promise God has for you until you forgive.

Laziness

The second reason for a spirit of poverty is laziness. Proverbs 24:33-34 says:

> *"Yet a little sleep, a little slumber, a little folding*
> *of the hands to sleep: So shall thy poverty come as one*
> *that travelleth; and thy want as an armed man."*

Is this verse saying you should sit back and wait for God to do everything for you? Do you think God is going to pour out His blessings on you while you're sitting there twiddling your thumbs? The Bible says, in James 2:18, "…I will shew thee my faith by my works."

You've got to be a doer of the Word and an activator of the Word. You've got to get out of the boat and walk on the water. You've got to begin to move forward. That's a vision, a prophetic utterance, to move forward. The lazy man who sits back and does nothing but dream, and never activates his dreams or works his dreams, will never receive the promises of God. Open your Bible to Joshua 1:8. It says:

> *"…thou shalt meditate therein day and night,*
> *that thou mayest observe to do according to all that is written*
> *therein: for then thou shalt make thy way prosperous,*
> *and then thou shalt have good success."*

Anything significant that happens in your life will happen because you sought out what God has for you.

Ecclesiastes 5:3 says:

"For a dream cometh through the multitude of business; and a fool's voice is known by multitude of words."

You can't just talk about your dreams. You must put forth effort!

Ignorance

The third reason for spiritual poverty is ignorance. Proverbs 24:4 tells us what happens when we find knowledge.

"And by knowledge shall the chambers be filled with all precious and pleasant riches."

The Bible also tells us what happens to us *without* knowledge. Hosea 4:6 says:

"My people are destroyed for lack of knowledge: because thou hast rejected knowledge, I will also reject thee, that thou shalt be no priest to me: seeing thou hast forgotten the law of thy God, I will also forget thy children."

Who does the Word say is destroyed for lack of knowledge? His people! Surely the Word doesn't mean people who love God! People who are going to church every Sunday! People who serve God! Yes, those people can also be destroyed by lack of knowledge. People can't receive deliverance and healing if they don't know they can be delivered and healed. We need to mine the treasures of God's Word so we can know how to walk by faith and how to believe for God's blessings for others and ourselves.

Now, turn in your Bible to Romans 12:2. It says:

"And be not conformed to this world: but be ye transformed by the renewing of your mind, that ye may prove what is that good, and acceptable, and perfect, will of God."

Notice that Paul says you prove the will of God by being *transformed through the renewing of your mind*—by making your mind *new*. You are to let the transforming power in the truths of Gods Word make your mind, emotions, and will brand new. If you neglect this power to be transformed, you will only continue to conform to the world's ways and the world's lies about who you are and who God is.

Pursue the Word. Pursue the truth. Learn it and then live it.

Oppressing the Poor

The fourth cause of spiritual poverty is oppression of the poor. Proverbs 22:16, 22 says:

"He that oppresseth the poor to increase his riches, and he that giveth to the rich, shall surely come to want. …Rob not the poor, because he is poor: neither oppress the afflicted in the gate…"

Watch how a man treats someone he needs. Then watch how he treats someone he *doesn't* need. You see, you don't know when God might send an angel disguised as someone dirty, someone you might pass by because you're wearing your nice, new suit and you don't want to get smelly or dirty. Would you take the time to say a kind word and offer support? Or would you turn your back to that person and oppress them? The poor need your kindness. God says if you oppress them, that oppression will bring you to a place of poverty and shame. This doesn't mean you should worry about every time you missed an opportunity to comfort someone. It means you should develop an attitude to be sensitive and non-judgmental toward all people.

God wants you to lend to the poor and take care of the poor. Understand that being poor is not just a financial condition. Being poor can be a spiritual or an emotional condition. It can be a physical condition. The poor are those who are without, who are in lack, who are depleted. If you take care of those who have need, God says you lend unto the Lord. God will recompense you again. He says he will bring you to a place of prosperity—perhaps even to a wealthy place.

Open your Bible to Luke 6:38. It says what?

> *"Give, and it shall be given unto you; good measure, pressed down, and shaken together, and running over, shall men give into your bosom. For with the same measure that ye mete withal it shall be measured to you again."*

What's the first word? Give! If you can't give, you can't quote the rest of the Scripture. If you give one ounce, you'll get back one ounce. If you give a cup, you'll get back a cup. If you give a gallon, you'll get back a gallon. *You* determine what is coming to you. You can't give an ounce and expect to get back a gallon.

The Bible is full of examples of how God loves to give. Ephesians 5:1 says, "Be ye therefore followers of God…" That means we should be like God and *love* giving. We need to imitate God when we give in love, in compassion, in respect, in money, and in all other things.

This leads you down a two-way street, though, and puts you on the *receiving* end. God loves receiving, too! He loves to receive your praise, your worship, your brokenness, your firstfruits, your love, your time.

You say you love to give, but can you graciously receive? If not, that could be pride. The reason you can be a cheerful giver and can't be a cheerful receiver is that when you *give*, you are in control. When you *receive*, you're *not* in control. Your willingness to receive must match up with your willingness to give. They go hand-in-hand.

If you get this teaching in your spirit, you'll be that much closer to understanding God's call on your life.

Misfortune

The fifth cause of spiritual poverty is misfortune. First Kings 17 tells the story of an afflicted woman. This story proves to us bad things sometimes do happen to good people. Fortunately, God's prophet ministered to the woman and she was delivered by faith from her misfortunes.

We may want to believe bad things should only happen to people who deserve them. But we know that's not true. There are things that will happen to everyone and it's simply misfortune. The Bible says the rain falls on the just and the unjust (Matthew 5:45). But, I've got good

Gospel news for you and it is perhaps the most comforting promise in the Bible. Romans 8:28 says:

"And we know that all things work together for good to them that love God, to them who are the called according to his purpose."

In other words, what the enemy means as your stumbling block, God will turn around and use as your steppingstone. You must know your misfortune is only for a season. God will pull you out of that pit and promote you to the palace because you love God and are called according to His purposes. He is sovereign and His plan and purpose will always be established in the obedient believer's life.

Withholding

The sixth cause of spiritual poverty is withholding. Proverbs 11:24-26 says:

"There is that scattereth, and yet increaseth; and there is that withholdeth more than is meet, but it tendeth to poverty. The liberal soul shall be made fat: and he that watereth shall be watered also himself. He that withholdeth corn, the people shall curse him: but blessing shall be upon the head of him that selleth it."

You may need to read this verse two or three times to fully grasp its meaning. It tells us that God blesses the person who gives. But those who hoard their increase or hold back from blessing others after they have been blessed will eventually fall into poverty themselves. As we read before, He says,

"Give, and it shall be given unto you; good measure, pressed down, and shaken together, and running over, shall men give into your bosom. For with the same measure that ye mete withal it shall be measured to you again" (Luke 6:38).

The person who holds back will "tendeth to poverty." If you are a giver, then your liberal (generous and giving) soul shall be made fat. This is also related to how you treat the poor. When you oppress the poor and withhold from giving to the poor, you are in prideful denial that God blesses you so you can be a blessing to others. It is God's nature to bless. And as His sons and daughters, He wants us to be like Him.

Taking Action

I would like for you to *think* about the six Biblical reasons for lack in your life. If you have committed any of these offenses, use them as a confession to God to wash your spirit clean. Psalm 32:1 says, *"Blessed is he whose transgression is forgiven, whose sin is covered."*

This verse goes on to say if you keep silent about your sin, your bones dry up. But if you have no guile (*guile* is an Old English word that means "sorcery") and you acknowledge your sin unto the Lord, the Word says, once again, you will be *blessed*.

In Conclusion

Remember, you can't conquer what you don't confront and you can't confront what you don't identify. You may have oppressed the poor but you can get yourself into alignment. You may have been stingy and greedy, but you can break the spirit of poverty in your life and stop withholding. Shut the door on poverty in your life and allow God to bring you to a place of prosperity by eliminating these six sins from your life.

Don't forget—prosperity is not just about money. Prosperity is a wholeness word that means nothing missing, nothing broken, nothing lacking in your life. Are you ready for that kind of increase in your life? I give you this instruction in order to prepare you for the next part of this book. Read on!

Part II

The Principle of Firstfruits

*"For if the firstfruit be holy, the lump is also holy:
and if the root be holy, so are the branches."*

(Romans 11:16)

One of the most important laws of the Bible involves the principle of *Firstfruits*. It is the law of first things first and it has a fundamental impact on everything in your life. Understanding and living by this law helps you position yourself to receive the promise God has for you.

Understanding the Principle of Firstfruits

Remember the third cause of spiritual poverty (page 22)? Ignorance. One of the biggest problems in the body of Christ is ignorance. What you don't know is crippling you. The Bible says, in James 3:16:

> *"For where envying and strife is, there is confusion and every evil work."*

Confusion means "disorder" and "every evil work in the spirit." The reason so many people are being attacked and are battling all kinds of unusual things is because they don't have the *order* of God. If you're battling stuff you don't understand, it may be caused by your lack of understanding of how first things (firstfruits) are either sanctified or cursed and how they establish what comes after it.

It's time to explore this principle of Firstfruits. Open your Bible to Leviticus 27:28-29. It refers to firstfruits as devoted to God:

> *"Notwithstanding no devoted thing, that a man shall devote unto the LORD of all that he hath, both of man and beast, and of the field of his possession, shall be sold*

or redeemed: every devoted thing is most holy unto the
LORD. None devoted, which shall be devoted of men,
shall be redeemed; but shall surely be put to death."

Before you read another word, you should
understand something—entire books could be written
about this single verse. I don't want you to get distracted
with trying to figure out what all this means. Right now,
I just want you to focus on what the Word is saying
about *devoted* things.

The Lord says every *devoted* thing is most holy unto
the Lord. *Devoted* is the same as firstfruit. First things are
holy things. Devoted things, first things, and firstfruits
all have the same meaning—it is the irrevocable giving
over to God. In other words, all first things belong to
God and any time you touch a first thing, you bring a
curse upon yourself. When you obey God and He sees
your heart is tender, He will show you the reason you've
been positioned to be blessed.

You'll see the strong hand of God favor you
and you'll see it because you obeyed the principle of
Firstfruits. Until you are faithful to this principle, you
can't complain about God not blessing you. God's Word
never fails!

Now go to Deuteronomy 8:17-18. It says:

"And thou say in thine heart, My power and the might
of mine hand hath gotten me this wealth. But thou shalt
remember the LORD thy God: for it is he that giveth thee

power to get wealth, that he may establish his covenant which he sware unto thy fathers, as it is this day."

This verse tells you to remember the *source* of the power that gives wealth. Once again, wealth isn't just a *money* term. It's a *wholeness* term that means protection, safety, security, and mental and financial stability.

Having this wholeness kind of wealth is within your power, but only if you are in confessed agreement with Deuteronomy 8:17-18. Remember it! Put it on your refrigerator! Say it a thousand times until you have it memorized! Remember the Lord thy God, for it is He that giveth thee power. *Power* means "an anointing, an ability." God has given you an anointing to get wealth and establish His covenant.

Here is the takeaway from Deuteronomy 8:18: Most people think the word *remember* means "to reference or to call forth from memory." Yes, the word *remember* usually means "to respect, reference, honor," but that's not what the Hebrew word used in Deuteronomy 8:18 means.

It says, "…thou shalt remember…" and *remember* here is the Hebrew word, *zakar. Zakar* is one of those rich Hebrew words like *Amen* that requires some knowledge of the covenants of God in order to fully understand. It is a powerful word that literally translates as "male of man" or "male of animal" or "to mark so as to be recognized to be male." In its covenant context, it harkens back to the mandate of God, in Exodus 13:1-2 below, to firstfruit unto Him every first male, human and animal, that opens the womb.

"And the LORD spake unto Moses, saying, Sanctify unto me all the firstborn, whatsoever openeth the womb among the children of Israel, both of man and of beast: it is mine."

God told Israel to sanctify, or set apart, for Him the male firstfruit of the womb. This was to acknowledge that God is the Lord of all.

FRAMEWORKS:
COVENANTAL HEADSHIP

A little background about covenantal headship will help you here. The covenantal head of a family, clan, tribe, church, or nation represents the whole before God. That's why the male heads of household brought burnt offerings to the temple. He offered for himself and his family. The High Priest of the temple was the covenantal head of the people before God. So it was he who entered the Holy of Holies once per year to offer the symbolic blood of atonement for himself and all the people of God. The covenantal head is set apart from what it represents. It is set apart for God. So, in the covenant context, to "zakar" (male) thy God is to regard Him as the Lord of all.

Everything owes its existence and its purpose to God, so He is the head of everything. "Remember thy God" is an everlasting covenant between God and His people. He is the God of all fruit that gives you the power to get wealth. And it is the people of God that sanctify, or set apart, the firstfruit for Him. He gives us power to establish His covenant. We give Him our firstfruits to, among other things, worship Him as Lord of ALL fruit. He gives it all.

After Moses delivered these words from God to the people (Exodus 13), he said to them (v.3):

"And Moses said unto the people, Remember this day, in which ye came out from Egypt, out of the house of bondage; for by strength of hand the LORD brought you out from this place: there shall no leavened bread be eaten."

Here, again, is the same word: *remember* (zakar). Moses now calls the people to firstfruit the week starting with that day in the month of Abib (roughly April) each year. The resulting feast was called Passover. It was a time to look back upon their deliverance from bondage in Egypt and a time to look forward to the future blessings as God's covenant people. Passover was the firstfruit (the head) of the year.

You have to get this in your spirit because I believe one of the biggest reasons we have not seen the wealth of God to establish His covenant in our lives is because we are pleading promises and breaking the principle of Firstfruits. It is the principle of one for many. It is the law that the first governs the rest. Until you position yourself with firstfruits, you cannot expect to possess God's promise.

The Fundamentals of Firstfruits

A *firstfruit* literally means "a promise to come." Whatever you do with firstfruits governs the rest and sets the pattern, or the promise, to come for the rest of whatever you establish. And first things always belong to God. In Genesis 22:2, God told Abraham, "Take now thy son, thine only son Isaac." First Corinthians 15:23 says, *"But every man in his own order: Christ the firstfruits; afterward they that are Christ's at his coming."* Romans 8:29 says, *"For whom he did foreknow, he also did predestinate to be conformed to the image of his Son, that he might be the firstborn among many brethren."* Jesus was the firstborn and thus He was the firstfruit.

God wanted a family, He sowed a Son. That's why Jesus ascended from hell. He said to Mary Magdalene, "Touch me not; for I am not yet ascended to my Father..." (John 20:17). He had to present Himself to God the Father as the firstfruit. Mary understandably wanted to grasp Jesus tightly and keep Him with her. But He had to be the spotless Lamb and without blemish. He couldn't be tarnished. He became the firstfruit offering so we might become sons of God.

Let's learn more about firstfruits in Exodus 13:11-13. It says:

"And it shall be when the LORD shall bring thee into the land of the Canaanites, as he sware unto thee and to thy fathers, and shall give it thee, That thou shalt set apart unto the LORD all that openeth the matrix, and every firstling that cometh of

a beast which thou hast; the males shall be the LORD'S. And every firstling of an ass thou shalt redeem with a lamb; and if thou wilt not redeem it, then thou shalt break his neck: and all the firstborn of man among thy children shalt thou redeem."

This verse is saying every firstborn thing is devoted to God in a covenantal way. In other words, when you get your breakthrough, when you get that increase at your job, when anything new is established in your life, you must acknowledge the source of that increase. The first of that whole increase is devoted to God.

The firstfruit is *not* a tithe of the increase. It's the *whole* increase. We'll examine the difference between the firstfruit and the tithe on page 39. What you must understand now is all first things belong to God, even the first part of your day. That's why the Bible says in Psalm 5:3:

"My voice shalt thou hear in the morning, O LORD; in the morning will I direct my prayer unto thee, and will look up."

The first of every thing belongs to God. He lays claim to it. Any time something is called a "first thing," a "firstfruit," a "devoted thing," God always lays claim to it because God sees the first thing as representing what comes after it. The principle is that God sees all things according to how the first things are treated. Romans 11:16 says:

"For if the firstfruit be holy, the lump is also holy: and if the root be holy, so are the branches."

FRAMEWORKS:
Christ the Firstfruit

The impact of Romans 11:16 goes deeper than any of us can comprehend. Jesus was God's first and only begotten son. He gave up His son to set Him apart as holy firstfruit. The firstfruit then sanctified all who came after so Jesus became the firstfruit of many brethren. This victory bought our redemption from the curse we inherited from our first father, Adam, who touched the firstfruit of the garden and took it into himself. The tree of the knowledge of good and evil was in the center of the garden. It was set apart unto God who alone declares things good or evil. The tree and its fruit were not evil, as some have assumed. The tree in the center was the firstfruit of the garden that represented the whole garden, which represented Eden, which represented the earth, which represented all of creation. No one was to touch the tree of God's knowledge and headship for their own use. Its fruit was the devoted thing Adam took for himself and brought a curse upon all of us. We inherited Adam's sin because he was the firstfruit of the family of man who represented us all. Let this bake for a while and you'll begin to grasp how fundamental the principle of Firstfruits is.

So, in essence, God says the first governs all the rest and if the first is holy, everything else will be holy. Are you thinking right now that the firstfruit is much more than you were taught to believe?

Let's go deeper still. Exodus 22:29-30 says:

"Thou shalt not delay to offer the first of thy ripe fruits, and of thy liquors: the firstborn of thy sons shalt thou give unto me. Likewise shalt thou do with thine oxen, and with thy sheep: seven days it shall be with his dam; on the eighth day thou shalt give it me."

Jesus fulfilled this old covenant way of obeying this mandate. We don't sacrifice the firstlings of our sheep at the temple anymore or redeem our firstborn sons with gold. Jesus paid for all needed redemption. But, the principle established by the Exodus mandate remains. Today, we dedicate all our children to God, pleading the blessings of His new covenant over them. It may be appropriate, however, to make a special offering to the storehouse of God for your firstborn child just to acknowledge that all your children are a gift from God.

God says first things belong to Him and He pursues covenant with first things to establish redeeming covenant with everything that comes after it. God said it is better to destroy a firstfruit than to use it for your own personal gain. If you touch a holy thing, it will bring a curse on you and God says it is better to destroy that thing rather than let it curse you.

Tithe vs. Firstfruits

The point of all this is that I believe the body of Christ has been misled. You may have been taught that firstfruit is your tithe. But your tithe is not your firstfruit.

Firstfruit is mentioned 32 times in the Bible. In Genesis 4, it is mentioned as "firstlings" or "firstfruits." Tithe is also mentioned 32 times in the Bible but your tithe is first mentioned when Abram pays his tithe to Melchizedek in Genesis 14:20. The firstfruit is different. I'll explain.

The tithe is the first tenth of God's daily provision (your regular paycheck or a bonus or any ordinary income or increase that comes as a regular part of God's provision for you). The firstfruit is the whole of something given to you by God that represents all that comes after it.

Let me give you an example. When I started this ministry, I received a substantial gift of money in support. Instead of using it to support the ministry, I firstfruited it to God in order to establish His covenant with the whole of my ministry. I gave the whole gift to Him and didn't use any of it in my own ministry. I believe this act of obedience is the reason my ministry prospers.

If the firstfruits are sanctified to God—relinquished to Him in some way that worships Him—then all that comes after will be blessed. But if the firstfruits aren't sanctified to God, then they are judged as withheld from Him and the fruit that comes after will be cursed. Proverbs 3:9-10 says,

"Honour the LORD with thy substance, and with the firstfruits of all thine increase: So shall thy barns be filled with plenty, and thy presses shall burst out with new wine."

God says your tithe and your firstfruits are not the same thing. The firstfruit is the first of every thing. After that, you tithe on everything else. I'm not just talking about your money either. I'm talking about your family, your time, your talent, your gifts. I'm talking about the first hours of your day, the first day of every week, the first month of every year, the first of everything that sanctifies all that follows. The first belongs to God and the first establishes the blessing or cursing of everything else.

In the Word, you will find that until you learn the Firstfruits principle, until you learn the principle of one for many, your life will be out of order. God will not bless disorder. Some of us learn this lesson the hard way.

The Lesson of Jericho

Do you remember the Battle of Ai recorded in Joshua 7? Just before this battle, the children of Israel crossed the Jordan River and arrived at Jericho to claim their first victory in the Promised Land. Jericho had the most sophisticated, successful army in the world. The wall surrounding the city was wide enough for three chariots to patrol on top of it, side by side. Jericho heard what God had done for Israel at the Red Sea but they proudly defied Israel and Israel's God. This passage about Jericho in Joshua 6 tells me your greatest warfare may be right before you enter your place of promise.

Here is the story. God gave the children of Israel a completely illogical battle plan: March around the walls of Jericho once a day for six days. On the seventh day, march around seven times and then "shout with a great shout" and blow the ram horns. March around the city and make noise—crazy instructions! But God promised the walls of Jericho would fall flat. And that is exactly what happened. The barrier Jericho built to keep out the children of Israel became a bridge! They had a major military victory there and God moved them on to Ai.

God will not bless disorder.

Now, taking Ai should have been a cake walk compared to Jericho. Ai was a small town with a few thousand fighting men. But what happened? The children of Israel got their rear ends kicked and the tiny town of Ai defeated them. How could this happen? Well, let's look at Joshua 7:1:

> *"But the children of Israel committed a trespass in the accursed thing: for Achan…of the tribe of Judah, took of the accursed thing: and the anger of the LORD was kindled against the children of Israel."*

FRAMEWORKS:
HOLY THINGS

Don't be confused when the Word says "accursed thing" some of the time and "holy" or "devoted thing" other times. Firstfruits are holy because they are to be devoted exclusively to our holy God. But understand that "holy" doesn't mean harmless. The holy things are the most dangerous. God is very, very dangerous. If not for our righteousness in Christ, there would be a great deal to tremble about.

But God is very, very good. This pure goodness and danger are the essence of holiness. So we dare not treat holy things as anything but holy because they carry with them a curse upon any defilement. Incidentally, God sees Christians as holy, too. Such a curse is upon any who would mistreat the least of us that it would be better for him or her to be cast into the sea tied to a millstone (Matthew 18:6).

Joshua 6:21 says this about Jericho: They "devoted the city to God." And verse 24 says they gathered the precious metals for the treasury of the Lord's house. The people knew Jericho was the firstfruit of the Promised Land. It was given by the obvious and strong hand of God. This meant Jericho was to be set apart and given up to God. Nothing from the city was to be taken as spoil for personal gain by anyone. But a leader of Israel under Joshua took gold, silver, and garments from Jericho and kept them for his own use. This man, Achan, touched the accursed thing. In other words, God held the children of Israel accountable because a holy thing had been defiled by Achan's personal use. The thing Achan took wasn't accursed because it came from Jericho, specifically. It was accursed because Jericho was the firstfruit and anything taken out of it was to be God's. Achan treated something from Jericho like it was his. This brought a curse upon him and all of Israel. When a few thousand of Israel's warriors suffered the humiliating defeat at Ai, Joshua ripped his clothes and beat his chest, crying on his face before God. He couldn't understand why God abandoned them. Look at verses 10 and 11:

> *"And the LORD said unto Joshua, Get thee up; wherefore liest thou thus upon thy face? Israel hath sinned, and they have also transgressed my covenant which I commanded them: for they have even taken of the accursed thing, and have also stolen, and dissembled also, and they have put it even among their own stuff."*

Notice how God asked Joshua, "Why are you on your knees, praying?" That's the position of a lot of Christians today. They're on their knees crying, "God, give me breakthrough! Give me blessings!" God is saying, "The heavens are shut to you! I'm not answering your prayers because you violated the principle of Firstfruits!" You can plead promises all day long but they do not bypass the principles of God.

There is hidden blessing in that, though. Most of us have walked out on the mercy of God because we were ignorant and didn't know what we were doing. God said to Joshua, "Get up from your knees and stop praying! Get things in order! For you have touched a holy and devoted thing and you have brought it among your own stuff!" God said, "You brought a firstfruit and mixed it in with your own stuff and now I can't move because you've handcuffed me!"

The reason you stand in authority and power is because He made you a son of the living God.

It's time for you to take the handcuffs off God. You have to get in order because first things belong to God. God didn't say, "Give me a tithe of Jericho." The whole thing belonged to God. That's why I dedicate the whole month of January to God. That's why you have to remember the Sabbath and keep it holy. It belongs to the Lord. That's why any time something is a first, it is holy. The whole part of that belongs to God and it governs the rest.

The Spirit of Revelation

If you've put your trust in Jesus and His victory to redeem you from the curse of Adam's sin, you're going to heaven and no weapon formed against you shall prosper (Isaiah 54:17). The reason you stand in authority and power is because He made you a son of the living God.

He became a firstfruit and firstfruit is a pattern. God is saying, "Get things in order because the blessing of the Lord is coming to you!" But if you aren't positioned properly, you won't be able to receive it. God wants to open your eyes according to Ephesians 1:17-18:

> *"That the God of our Lord Jesus Christ, the Father of glory, may give unto you the spirit of wisdom and revelation in the knowledge of him: The eyes of your understanding being enlightened; that ye may know what is the hope of his calling, and what the riches of the glory of his inheritance…"*

The spirit of revelation means you will understand the mystery of the inheritance—that you can know what God has for you—and that you don't have to walk through life in a spirit of poverty.

Remember the principle of Firstfruits. Get it in order and He will give you power to get wealth and to be whole in your mind, in your marriage, in your finances, and in your body so that He may establish His covenant with you.

In Conclusion

First things first. That's why the Bible says to remember the Lord thy God. Firstfruit the Lord thy God. That same Hebrew word, *zakar*, is found when Noah was spared. The Word says the Lord remembered. The Lord firstfruited Noah for His covenant's sake (Genesis 8:1). It says to remember the Sabbath and keep

it holy. Zakar (firstfruit) the Sabbath and keep it holy.
It's God's day.

I know you have a lot to do that day. But it's not your
shopping day. It's not your family entertainment day. It's
not your play day. It's a holy day and you firstfruit it to
the Lord. Do this and all your days will be holy in God's
eyes.

What you do first thing in the morning sets the rest
of the day. You don't need to get up, get your coffee,
and start doing your own thing. You need to say, "Good
morning, Holy Spirit. I bless You today." You need to
worship your Lord and hear from Him. Then, get *your*
day going.

Now that you understand the principle of Firstfruits,
it's time to teach you about seedtime and harvest. It's
time to learn about planting your seed in the kingdom
and taking possession of God's promise through His
perpetual system of sowing and reaping.

Part III

God's System of Seedtime and Harvest

"While the earth remaineth, seedtime and harvest, and cold and heat, and summer and winter, and day and night shall not cease."

(Genesis 8:22)

What is it that God has promised you? Is it a glorious and great future? Is it a strong anointing to see nations shaken by the power of God? Is it that you will be the head and not the tail? Is it that you will be blessed in the city and blessed in the field? And that your children will rise up and call you blessed? Whatever your promise is, He is faithful to fulfill it.

Taking Possession of the Promise

"And the LORD said unto Abram, after that Lot was separated from him, Lift up now thine eyes, and look from the place where thou art northward, and southward, and eastward, and westward: For all the land which thou seest, to thee will I give it, and to thy seed for ever" (Genesis 13:14).

These verses concern a promise God gave to our father, Abraham, who was then called Abram. He had been given the *promise*, his whole life was pregnant with it, but he didn't have *possession*.

You may be in the same situation today. You may be pregnant with a promise from God's Word or His revealed will in your life, but you do not have possession of it. In this section, I am going to teach you how to take possession of that promise and how to begin functioning victoriously in the kingdom of God and see all He has promised come to pass for you. But for you to understand how to function in His kingdom, you must first understand God's system of operation.

Seeing the Kingdom of God

While many of us pray for more faith, I do not believe more faith is what we need. We need to know how to properly apply the faith God has given us.

It is possible for you to live your entire life and never take possession of what God has promised you. What a tragedy to merely exist and never fulfill one's destiny!

We could spend our lifetime learning about this part of our glory in Jesus. But aren't you glad we don't have to know and understand all of God's mysteries to move forward in faith and expectation? God teaches us line upon line, precept upon precept.

Growing Christians always hunger for God to reveal more of Himself. But growing Christians who walk with the Spirit in triumph over their circumstances don't wait for more lines and precepts before standing on the Truth they already possess. They strive to be of one mind with God. But there are plenty of people out there who don't care about being of one mind with God.

Let me ask you this: Are you fighting with relatives and other people who don't understand you? Do they ask, "Why are you going to church every Sunday? Why are you bringing your tithe to the house of God? Why are you giving your time to missions work?" Jesus reveals the answer in John 3:3:

"Jesus answered and said unto him, Verily, verily, I say unto thee, Except a man be born again, he cannot see the kingdom of God."

He says a man must be born again or he cannot *see* the kingdom of God. The Greek word translated *see* means "understand, have revelation, comprehend." He cannot *comprehend* the kingdom, or the system, of God. Your unsaved friends and relatives just don't understand why you do what you do. And you can't begin to articulate it to them because the god of their world blinds them. They cannot have revelation, comprehension, or understanding of why you do what you do. The reason is simple and terrifying: The world's system is totally different from God's system. The world says, "Get, get, get." But God says, "Give, give, give." The world says, "Step on somebody…Sleep your way to the top…Manipulate." God says, "You have to *die*, flesh, in order to truly live!" You have to *decrease* in order to *increase*. Humble yourself and He will exalt you in due season. You can't be double-minded and *see* the kingdom of God.

Some Simple Truths

The body of Christ is full of what James called "the double-minded" (1:8). They say with their lips what they know in their minds to be true. But when given the opportunity to stand on it, they act like unbelievers. They doubt, they hesitate, they try to find another way to control the situation, and they never give God a chance to show Himself strong. How can God do anything for such a person? He would get no glory if He did and the person wouldn't grow an inch. What's more, it's an insult to the glory of God not to act on what one knows is true.

The simplest truths are the greatest and we can't go any further into the Word about seedtime and harvest until we examine these most basic precepts about faith. If you don't get these and commit yourself to them, then learning more precepts about taking possession of the promise won't help you. That's because you'll be living like a double-minded Christian until you get it and commit to it. It takes commitment and endurance to be single-minded.

Faith Is Acting on What We Know and Trust

Faith comes by hearing and hearing by the Word of God (Romans 10:17). It is through hearing and receiving the Truth that faith makes its journey to our hearts. The Word can't become faith if it just enters our ears and then camps out in our minds. But that's where it stays until we act on the Truth we've heard, understood, and believed. It costs nothing to pack our minds full of principles and knowledge. But it takes commitment to have fulfilled possession of God's promise.

You don't have to understand all the events and forces at work in your life. You just have to agree with God. You must know with confidence God's Word is true and you must speak and act consistently in ways that confess your commitment to the Truth regardless of what the world or your circumstances say.

Here's an example everyone faces: Life can be hard, people can be nasty, and you can lose things precious to you. But as a Christian, you should already know God is holy, faithful, and good—even if your life at present

doesn't feel good—even if your life never feels as good
as you want it to feel. God is good—period. That's the
Truth. But if you hold grudges against people, fill your
prayers with whining, or measure God's goodness by your
circumstances, you aren't walking in faith that God is
good.

Do you remember the story of Job? Job lost and
suffered more than any man we can find in the Bible. He
was so anguished, he cursed the day he was born. But
even at his lowest point, he never accused God. He said,
"Though he slay me, yet will I trust in him" (Job 13:15).

God Never Fails to Fulfill His Promise

If you have a vision for a ministry and God has
confirmed it is His will for you, then you have His promise
of fulfillment. God has planted that promise into you. Now
you must speak and act consistently with your assurance
that God is faithful. And if you endure to speak and
act according to Truth, your promise will become your
possession.

The seed of faith will grow into fruit in its season. But
if you become impatient or unsatisfied with the way God is
bringing fulfillment, you will bring weeds into the harvest.
Even Abraham was capable of weak faith in the face of
God's faithfulness. He lost patience in God's promise
of a son and took matters into his own hands. Today in
the Middle East, we see the tragic results of Abraham's
mistake.

Abraham should have continued to declare things that
aren't as though they are (Romans 4:17). God's promise

makes unseen things a present reality. The unseen things exist as the substance of our faith and our faith says nothing can stop it. Nothing can interfere with what God has called forth.

When Peter saw Jesus walking on the Sea of Galilee to join him and the other disciples in their boat, he asked the Lord to call him out to join Him on the water. He didn't just step out on his own. He waited for Jesus to answer his vision with a promise. Peter knew his miracle-working Lord was faithful. He knew if Jesus called him, he too would walk on the water. Jesus told Peter to come to Him and Peter responded to the call as a promise of fulfillment. He seized possession of His Lord's promise and took a few steps on the water. But then something happened. Peter became distracted by the tossing waves and took his eyes off the Truth and the Lord's promise. He began to sink as he responded in fear and doubt to his circumstances (Matthew 14:22-33).

The greatness to which God calls you can only be robbed from you by your own unbelief—unbelief expressed through fear, doubt, or disobedience.

You can't expect to take possession of what God has *not* promised in His word or in His calling for you. You need to know what God has promised, keep your eyes on it, confess it, and act on it without being distracted by unbelief. Your circumstances have no impact upon the Truth. But how confidently and consistently you respond to the Truth will have an impact on your circumstances.

Incidentally, God will fulfill His own purposes no matter what you do or don't do. He is like a fast moving locomotive heading for Home. Wouldn't it be great to be on that train instead of waiting at the station?

We Have Access to God's Kingdom

Access to God's kingdom is our inheritance in Jesus. Whatever God calls into our lives, no matter how seemingly out of reach, is ours to possess if we will believe. Of course life is devastating sometimes. But it is we who allow life circumstances to stand in the way of our future and our promise.

Jesus said when a seed is sown it dies, but then it emerges with new life. Having access to the kingdom involves death and resurrection, as well. Jesus was the seed sown that died but then emerged with fruit-bearing life. Through Jesus, old things are swept away and all things are made new by the power of His death and resurrection. Everything into which Jesus is allowed to enter can be made new by the same power that raised Him from the dead.

That means *you* can be made new. Accepting Jesus as your Savior is the first step. This is your first access point to the kingdom. Then the Holy Spirit will teach you how to continually follow Jesus. He will never leave you even though there may be times when you drift and lose sight of Him. The world's system can cloud your vision and lead you away from the life-changing resurrection power of Jesus. The principles you will learn in this book will help you to resist the world's lies and stay close to the Truth.

The Seven Principles of Seedtime and Harvest

Now let's look at God's Word and examine more deeply the basic principles that will help you to take possession of the promise God has given you. This teaching is based on Genesis 13:14-17.

"And the LORD said unto Abram, after that Lot was separated from him, Lift up now thine eyes, and look from the place where thou art northward, and southward, and eastward, and westward: For all the land which thou seest, to thee will I give it, and to thy seed for ever. And I will make thy seed as the dust of the earth: so that if a man can number the dust of the earth, then shall thy seed also be numbered. Arise, walk through the land in the length of it and in the breadth of it; for I will give it unto thee."

Leave and Cleave

Genesis 13:14 says:

"And the LORD said unto Abram,"

We should get excited when we read that verse because Abram was Abraham's pre-covenant name. Joshua reveals that Abram served strange gods. So, God was giving a promise to a man with a heathen background. This tells us God did not look at Abram's background. God did not consider his *past* in determining his *future*.

The Bible teaches us eternal Truth and shows us God's power and faithfulness without hiding the shortcomings of the people He chose to work through and bless. Be grateful for this because if God could see beyond their flaws and failures to use them, then He can see beyond yours and use *you* for His purposes.

This means you need to forget those things behind you and press toward the mark of the high calling (Philippians 3:14). It means God has better things in front of you than those that are behind you. That sets you free. What a glorious God we serve!

> *"And the LORD said unto Abram, after that Lot was separated from him,"*

To begin taking possession of what God has promised, you have to separate yourself from things that are incompatible with the promise of God. Abram's nephew, Lot, was living with Abram and represented an attachment to Abram's heathen past. In Genesis 12:1, God told Abram to leave his past behind him. But like many of us, he tried to drag his past into his present. Abram was slow to recognize that Lot was tying him to the past and keeping him from moving forward in God's promise.

The first principle you must understand and commit to, if you are going to possess your promise, is *leave and cleave*. You have to leave yesterday in the past, leave all doubt about God's goodness, leave all self-centered thoughts about your worthiness or unworthiness, leave negative, defeated thinking, leave all fear of the future, and leave all the bondages of sin. Cleave to your tomorrow. Cleave to the Word of God. Cleave to what God has promised you.

When a man leaves his mother and cleaves to his wife, he becomes one flesh with her. In much the same way, Abraham became one with God's words of promise so that he forsook all other words.

Now you must forsake all words and deeds that contradict God's Word. Leave what is behind you and cleave to what is before you.

When Lot finally separated from Abram, God began to speak to Abram. Likewise, there are some things God cannot talk to you about until you are willing to remove Lot (your past and your disobedience) from your life.

You must leave your past behind you. Cleave to what is promised.

Change Your Focus

Genesis 13:14 continues:

"Lift up now thine eyes, and look from the place where thou art northward, and southward, and eastward, and westward…"

You may be waiting for God to change your situation and circumstances. But God says, "I'm not going to change your situation. I'm going to give you revelation and I will give you the spirit to believe it, stand on it, and rest in it until your situation matches your revelation." That is why the Bible declares in Romans 4:17 that you should call those things which *are not* as though they *are*. Although God may choose to keep you in your situation, your perspective—your attitude and perception—can change and that revelation will release you into the will of God.

God says, "Lift up your eyes right from where you are." You want God to rescue you from your mess, but God wants you to change your perception right in the middle of your mess. Yes, God does have a system and He says, "Stop looking at your condition and your sorry situation and lift up your eyes and look from the very place where you are now."

So, lift up your eyes! In Ecclesiastes 11:4, the Bible declares that he who regards the wind does not sow and he who regards the clouds does not reap. In other words, if you are always looking at the natural conditions (your current situation), you will never be a part of God's system. You are too distracted by the wind and the clouds to keep your eyes on Jesus. Your mouth is too full of unbelieving words to speak any agreement with Jesus. Your perception of your situation is not in alignment with God's perception.

How do you change your perception? By changing your position. Stop looking down. Stop looking at what's wrong. Stop looking at your mess. Stop seeing your husband as someone who doesn't love you and begin to see him as the high priest of your household. Stop looking at the only two pennies you have to rub together and begin to see that God gives you the power to obtain wealth and establish His covenant according to Deuteronomy 8:18:

> *"But thou shalt remember the LORD thy God: for*
> *it is he that giveth thee power to get wealth…"*

Lift up your head and look beyond your heartache, your bank account, and your sorry situation. You are going to die in the darkness if you do not lift up your head and see a new dawn on the horizon. It may be dark now, but there is a new day dawning. Every morning God gives you another chance—a chance to fight forward, to pass the test, to conquer the mountain before you, to move in the faith He has given to you, to see His promise of better days before you.

God told Abram to lift up his eyes *from where he was*. If you can change your position then you can change your perception, and perception determines your possession. Perception is essential for your possession because perception is more powerful than reality. It is not what *is* that influences the future—it is what is *perceived to be*.

Vision: If You Can See It, You Can Receive It

Genesis 13:15 says:

> *"For all the land which thou seest, to thee will*
> *I give it, and to thy seed for ever."*

Once you commit to change your perception from a focus on your circumstances to a focus on what God says, the next thing you must do is have a clear vision of the promise. You have to see the promise in order to receive it. You cannot have it unless you can see it.

Vision produces the desire to move forward. It is the prophetic utterance, the voice of God. Proverbs 29:18 declares that without vision, the people perish. Your soul dies without the vision of God.

"Having made known unto us the mystery of his will, according to his good pleasure which he hath purposed in himself" (Ephesians 1:9).

The power to change comes when hidden things are made manifest (known) to you. God gives you the power to change. He gives you the power to move forward and to be released from the bondage of your past. He gives you the revelation you need to change and He gives you the ability to change. He makes known to you His will and His purpose in your life.

Isaiah 46:10 talks about vision. It says God will make known the end from the beginning. He shows it to you. He gives you a glimpse of your future for you to possess it.

Remember this: Before you can take possession of the promise, you must have this vision. You must see it to receive it. Once you can see it, then you become pregnant with the promise.

Understand the Purpose for the Storm

The next principle for obtaining possession of God's promise lies in being prepared for the storm.

When you receive revelation, or a word from God, you must be ready for an attack by the enemy. Whenever you get ready to act on what God has put in you, the enemy will always bring distractions.

Mark 4:15 declares that immediately after the Word of God is sown, Satan comes. The Bible declares persecution will arise for the Word's sake. (We'll talk more about persecution on Page 67.)

So, the moment you become pregnant with that promise (you can see it, your perception has changed, and you have revelation), the enemy can't wait to bring in a distraction. Distraction is meant to break your focus because people with a broken focus fail in life. It isn't mentioned in Matthew, but I would bet it was the enemy that distracted Peter from focusing on Jesus and His promise when he failed to walk to Jesus on the water. The devil probably shouted into his thoughts something like, "Are you crazy? What are you thinking? You're not the Messiah! Do you want to drown? Look at these waves!" I would also bet you hear things like that whenever you try to move forward from disparaging circumstances in your life. That's because the devil wants nothing more than to keep you in a prison.

The distraction is your storm but you must understand there is a purpose for your storm. Hebrews 6:12 says the promises are inherited through your faith and your patience. But your faith may not be the promise. Faith comes by the Word of God (Romans 10:17) and produces a vision. Once God gives you a vision and deposits it in your spirit, you know God is faithful. You know you are the head and not the tail. You know your spouse is going to be saved and your children are going to rise up and call you blessed. You know God is going to heal you. You know God is going to explode your ministry and foundations are going to be shaken.

The challenge is not in the faith—the challenge is often in the *patience*. James 1:2-4 declares:

"My brethren, count it all joy when you fall into divers temptations, knowing this, that the trying of your faith worketh patience. But let patience have her perfect work, that ye may be perfect and entire, wanting nothing."

Let's look at this verse a little closer and discover exactly what it is saying.

Verse	Meaning
My brethren, count	to command with authority
it all joy	calm delight
when you fall into	to be caught by
divers temptations	different trials, tests, and attacks
knowing this, that the trying of your faith	the Word inside of you, the vision God has put inside you
worketh patience. But let patience have	ability to stand, undistracted
her perfect work, that ye may be perfect	complete
and entire,	whole like Jesus
wanting nothing.	no spiritual deficit or compromise

You might say, "How does that happen, Pastor Paula?" Hebrews 10:36 says you have need of patience. Many people say you should not pray for patience but the Bible says you *need* patience, "that after ye have done the will of God, ye might receive the promise."

In other words, you need patience in order to do the will of God and once you do the will of God, the promise comes. So how does patience come?

"And not only so, but we glory (God's praises and integrity come forth) *in tribulations also: knowing that tribulation worketh patience; and patience, experience; and experience, hope"* (Romans 5:3, 4).

Whenever you get ready to deliver what God has put in you, the enemy sends a storm. But what the enemy has meant for bad, according to Romans 8:28, God is turning it around and using it for good. The same storm the enemy sends to distract and destroy you is the storm God will use to develop patience in your life so you can inherit the promise.

You'll know you have acquired the spirit of patience when the focus of your soul is transformed from self-preservation and personal peace to Christ glorification and kingdom peace. Jesus is our Healer and a whole body is one promise of your inheritance in Jesus. But Jesus wants to give you more than just a whole body so you can live more comfortably. He wants to give you a spirit of such trust in Him, you are willing to look foolish while you shout your prayer, "Lord glorify Yourself in this broken body! Let the world worship You for Your power to heal and put them to shame who mock Your promises!" I believe God finds such self-abandoning faith and focus on Jesus irresistible.

Psalm 46:1 says:

"God is our refuge and strength, a very present help in trouble."

You will find the power of God in your time of trouble. The Bible declares in 2 Corinthians 12:9, ". . . for my strength is made perfect in weakness." In your weakness, His strength is made perfect! John 9 shows us that, at least sometimes, infirmity comes into our lives for no other reason than for the works of God to be manifested in them and thus glorify Him.

Whenever you get ready to deliver what God has put in you, the enemy sends a storm.

The disciples wondered if the man in John 9 was blind because of his or his parent's sins. Jesus showed them that it was neither. He was blind so God could be glorified when he was healed. Now for all eternity, that man will be crying out, "Guess what?! That was me Jesus healed! Who would have thought God would glorify Himself through a pitiful, broken creature like me?" How can a few years of infirmity compare with that kind of eternal rejoicing? And you know he would be willing to go through it all again.

There is a purpose for the storm in your life. Don't let the devil bring that distraction to destroy you. Let God use that storm to build your patience and endurance, which brings us to the fifth principle.

Endurance: It Takes Commitment

"Blessed is the man that endureth temptation: for when he is tried, he shall receive the crown of life, which the Lord hath promised to them that love him" (James 1:12).

If you are going to take possession of your promise, you must endure. You are rewarded only for that which you endure in life. And to endure takes commitment. That's difficult because many people do not want to stand. Matthew 24:13 says:

"But he that shall endure unto the end, the same shall be saved."

The prize is not given to those who run fast at the beginning of the race, but it is given to those who *endure*. Reward comes as a result of your endurance.

To *endure* means "to continue in the same state without perishing, to last, to remain firm, as under suffering, and to suffer patiently." It means "to stand firm under pressure." The Bible declares in James 1:6-8:

"But let him ask in faith, nothing wavering. For he that wavereth is like a wave of the sea driven with the wind and tossed. For let not that man think that he shall receive any thing of the Lord. A double minded man is unstable in all his ways."

The reason we often do not possess that which God has promised us is because we are in, we are out, we are unstable, we are inconsistent—we are double minded. We talked about being double-minded earlier in this section.

We believe God on Monday but we forfeit the promise by Friday when we get flaky in our commitment to the Truth.

When I contracted a lung disease and my lungs began to operate as low as twenty-eight percent, my situation did not match up to my revelation. I knew God is Jehovah Rapha, the God that healeth thee. The enemy would have loved for me to get flaky in my theology but it did not matter if I went to the grave. I still believed God is a healer. No matter what my situation said, I still believed

When the doctors said it was impossible, I knew the Word of God was higher than any natural law.

God is a healer. When the doctors used words like "incurable" and "impossible," I stood on the Word of God. I spoke to my situation. I called these lungs whole. I pronounced the Word of God, according to Isaiah 55:11, *"it shall not return unto me void, but it shall accomplish that which I please, and it shall prosper in the thing whereto I sent it."*

I spoke to my body and I commanded that it be healed by the blood covenant of Jesus Christ because *"he was wounded for our transgressions, he was bruised for our iniquities: the chastisement of our peace was upon him; and with his stripes we are healed"* (Isaiah 53:5).

I personalized that verse and said, "He was wounded for MY transgressions. He was bruised for MY iniquity. With His stripes, I AM healed." I expected to be healed, but I didn't need it to prove to me who God is and all I have in Jesus. I didn't need proof. I had the Word. That Word worked in my life when doctors gave a negative prognosis. When the doctors said it was impossible, I knew the Word of God was higher than any natural law. I stood firm under pressure. I *endured*.

You can also endure. Do not forfeit God's promise in your life. It takes commitment to see possession. You must believe God and be consistent in that belief.

> *"And Jesus answered and said, Verily I say unto you, There is no man that hath left house, or brethren, or sisters, or father, or mother, or wife, or children, or lands, for my sake, and the gospel's, But he shall receive an hundredfold now in this time, houses, and brethren, and sisters, and mothers, and children, and lands, with persecutions; and in the world to come eternal life"* (Mark 10:29-30).

You see, God promised us that for anything we leave or anything we give up in this lifetime for the Gospel's sake, we will receive a hundredfold in return. If He said it, it must come into your life. However, He also said it would come with persecution.

The promise is often packaged with persecution and that is why you have to make a decision—a decision to be committed, a decision to be consistent, a decision to stand firm on what God has said, even when the situation seems contrary to the promise. You must say, "I have decided to follow Jesus." And with that kind of tenacity, you will see God's promise fulfilled in your life.

But don't think of persecution as the price you pay for God's promise. It's definitely not! Jesus already paid for your place in the kingdom.

Be careful, too, not to let the devil tempt you to pride for your endurance. You insult the Cross by thinking you can add anything to it by enduring persecution. No, Jesus warned us we would face persecution because He did, and we are not better than our Master. It is a privilege to enter the battle for the kingdom. Persecution is our invitation to fight our true enemy with God's Word.

Learn to Operate in God's System

Once you are consistently living by these principles, you'll discover you have the ability to receive because you can perceive and know what God has promised. You realize the storm and the distractions are trying to make you forfeit the Word of God and you've made the commitment to stand firm on the Word. The most important thing now is to learn how to function and operate in God's system.

What do I mean by "the system"? When God gives you a word—a promise—there is a system of operation. How we possess that promise and how we possess what God has declared in our lives is determined by how we operate the system of faith.

There are two systems in operation right now—the world system and the system known as the kingdom of God. Everything in your life is operating in one system or the other.

The world system is the way the world operates. Even though you are *in* this world, you are not *of* this world.

Jesus said, "Repent; for the kingdom of heaven is at hand" (Matthew 4:17). The kingdom of God—God's way of doing things—is a system or a method of operation. What most people call faith is not faith at all; it is just high expectation based on wrong information. Real faith is the *Word*. Romans 10:17 says, "*. . .faith cometh by hearing, and hearing by the word of God.*" No Word—no faith. You cannot just *have* faith, you must *operate in* faith. This is where most people miss it because faith has to operate within God's system. Again, you have to be a doer of the Word.

In every area of our lives, the Bible tells us how to operate. For instance, your marriage is either operating on what the world has to say in its latest book on how to operate your marriage and how to conduct your lifestyle, or it is operating according to the Word of God. The Word of God tells wives to submit to their husbands and husbands to love their wives as Christ loved the church.

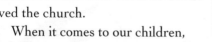

Persecution is our invitation to fight our true enemy with God's Word.

When it comes to our children, we follow the 32 ways the world tells us to discipline (or not to discipline) and raise our children. But the Bible has very clear instruction—"*Train up a child in the way he should go* (and it tells us the way he should go) *and when he is old, he will not depart from it* (Proverbs 22:6).

The Bible also tells us how to handle our money. The world says we should save, save, save—save for a rainy day; take care of me, me, me. But the Word of God declares in Luke 6:38, *"Give, and it shall be given unto you; good measure, pressed down, and shaken together, and running over, shall men give into your bosom."* Go back to Part I and the Six Biblical Reasons for Lack in Your Life (Page 18) if you need to be refreshed about what happens to your spirit if you oppress the poor by keeping everything for yourself.

Nobody seeks just for the sake of seeking.

You can love God with all of your heart and you can be a strong Christian, but still operate part of your life on the wrong system based on worldly principles. If you're knowingly doing this, you are saying to God, "Lord, I love You and I want You to bless me but I don't want to look weird. When it comes to my kids or my job or most other things, I'd rather stick with what I'm doing." I believe this kind of self-centered unbelief is why we do not see the promise of God manifest in our lives to the extent we should.

So let's learn how to operate the system God has given us in the Word. Remember—everything in your life is operating on either the *world's* system or *God's* system.

"Therefore take no thought, saying, What shall we eat? or, What shall we drink? or, Wherewithal shall we be clothed? (For after all these things do the Gentiles seek) for your heavenly Father knoweth that ye have need of all these things" (Matthew 6:31-32).

This Scripture says do not give any thought to what you are going to eat, what you are going to drink, or how you are going to be clothed. You may be thinking, *Wait a minute, God, those are important things!*

The Bible says the Father (your heavenly Father) knows you have need of all these things. So, if God knows your need, what is the *master key* to your need being met? You are not even supposed to take thought of those things! They are not even supposed to occupy your time or your mind. And yet most people are waking up early and getting home late, just to get a paycheck to take care of these basic necessities of life and they are not fulfilling their destiny. Help us, Jesus!

Let's break this down a little more to get you deep into it.

The Master Key: Seek First the Kingdom of God

The master key is found in Matthew 6:33:

"But seek ye first the kingdom of God, and his righteousness; and all these things shall be added unto you."

Righteousness here means "covenant rights." So the *master key* is to seek first the kingdom of God. It is noble for someone to be willing to do whatever it takes to provide for a family. The problem is most people who toil endlessly aren't just trying to provide. They're seeking security they don't know or don't believe they can have as a child of God.

If we seek first the kingdom of God and His righteousness instead of our own, it is a promise that everything we need to live, be productive, and have joy will be added to our lives. That is simple—and fantastic! Just seek first the kingdom of God and all those things are provided.

So, if that is the case, then we need to find out exactly what the kingdom of God is because seeking, in itself, is a frustrating process! Nobody seeks just for the sake of seeking. Whatever we are seeking, we must be desperate enough and determined enough to push through every barrier in order to obtain that which we are seeking.

What Is the Kingdom?

The word *kingdom* means "The dominion of the king." The kingdom of God is a method—God's way of doing things. It's His methodology.

> *"And Jesus looked round about, and saith unto his disciples, How hardly shall they that have riches enter into the kingdom of God!"* (Mark 10:23).

Let's break down this verse. Jesus was not talking about going to Heaven when He referred to the entering of the kingdom. (Remember, there are two systems in operation.) In other words, He was saying how hard it is for the rich man to enter into God's way of doing things—not into Heaven, but into the methodology of God. Verse 24 says:

> *"And the disciples were astonished at his words. But Jesus answereth again, and saith unto them, Children, how hard is it for them that trust in riches to enter into the kingdom of God!"*

His disciples were astonished at His words! It is very difficult for a self-made man—a rich man who has made it in this world's system by doing things his own way and through his own logic—to turn around, die to that system, lay it down, and pick up God's methods. Why do some rich men have a trust issue with God? They can't seek God's kingdom first if it means God might take everything away in order to redirect their lives. It wouldn't have to come to that if their hearts could become surrendered to God any other way. But a rich man typically trusts himself and his material resources most. And once you're in that position, it's hard to unlearn it.

Operating in the Kingdom

The methods of God are quite contrary to the world's methods. Remember, Romans 8:7 says the carnal, or natural, mind is enmity with God. All the logic and brilliance of our natural minds are still in opposition to God's ways. In fact, whenever God gets ready to release you into greatness He usually gives you very illogical instructions because He does things that are not based on human logic. That is why the Bible declares in Proverbs 4:7 that we should, in all our getting, "get understanding." Get yourself the wisdom and the knowledge of God.

Jesus preached that the kingdom of God—God's way of doing things—had come and He advised people to repent. Repenting is not saying, "I'm sorry I got caught." To repent means to turn your direction and change your way of doing things. Change the way you have operated your life because the kingdom of God—God's way of doing things—has come.

We established in Part I of this book that people who don't operate in God's system can't understand why you do the things you do. The answer, as you recall, is found in John 3:3:

If you have authority to plant seed, you have the power to make decisions.

> *"Jesus answered and said unto him, Verily, verily, I say unto thee, Except a man be born again, he cannot see* (comprehend, understand and have revelation of) *the kingdom of God."*

That is why they don't understand. They do not understand Leviticus 27:30 tells us the tithe is holy and it belongs to the Lord. You bring your tithe into the storehouse because, according to Malachi 3:8, you will not be a thief who robs God. That is God's system.

Tithing is a holy covenant. It establishes covenant. It opens up the windows of Heaven and pours out so great a blessing there will not be room enough to receive it. It makes you a delightsome land. It rebukes the devourer (Malachi 3:10-12). But those who do not believe will never understand this.

They also do not understand why you come to church week after week, even though the Bible says we should not forsake the assembling of ourselves together and even more so as we see the day approaching (Hebrews 10:25).

They do not understand why you forgive when you have been wronged, even though the Bible tells us we are to forgive "seventy times seven" in a day (Matthew 18:22), and when we are struck on one cheek, we are to turn the other (Matthew 5:39).

The Bible declares the first thing you must do to operate in the system of God is to be born again. Without the new birth, you will not *see, comprehend, understand, or have revelation of* God's way of doing things.

So what is His way? In chapter four of Mark, Jesus taught the disciples a parable which would open up all the parables of the kingdom. If they understood the first one, it would guide them to an understanding of everything else.

FRAMEWORKS:
THE KEY TO THE PARABLES

The parable Jesus shared with His disciples was the parable of the sower and the seed (Mark 4). Jesus compared the kingdom of God to the planting of seeds. The sower of the seed, He said, doesn't understand what makes the seed grow and he knows it certainly isn't him that makes things grow. And yet he knows he will have no crop unless he sows seed. And when he sows he knows the seed that falls on good soil will sprout and grow. He knows when the crop matures it is time to harvest. He sows, he watches, and then he reaps the harvest. It is the same for us when we sow the Word of

God. We sow the Word into the world and those who receive it like good soil will grow spiritually. When we sow the Word into our own life situations, we too must be good soil. We must receive the Word, put our trust in it, and watch for the harvest—expect it. Like the sower, we don't have to fully understand how God gives us our harvest. We just do the sowing, watching, and reaping.

Authority and Seed

It's time to get to the heart of this book. Up to this point, you have learned how important it is to position yourself to receive God's promise. You know God wants to bless you and you know the Word is your covenant. You also understand the six Biblical reasons for lack in your life. You learned the fundamental principle of Firstfruits so you understand the first governs the rest. And you learned the difference between the world's system of operation and God's system of operating in the kingdom.

The Promise of Dominion

Now is the time to learn about the planted seed and your authority to sow the seed. Open your Bible to Genesis 1:26. It says:

> *"And God said, Let us make man in our image, after our likeness: and let them have dominion…"*

God gave mankind many gifts. One of them is dominion (authority) to sow the seed. Verse 29 says:

*"And God said, Behold, I have given you
every herb bearing seed…"*

Someone might say, "Yes, but we lost that dominion when man fell into sin." Jesus regained that dominion for us when He was crucified on an old rugged cross, buried in a borrowed tomb, and rose again on the third day. He gave back to us the seed of the kingdom and He gave us the authority to plant the seed in His name.

Authority to Sow

What can you do with authority? What can you do with seed? If you have authority to plant seed, you have the power to make decisions. And the outcome of those decisions is only limited by your courage to plant and your faithfulness in tending the crop.

If you have seed and authority, you do not have to wait for someone to give you a big break in life. The principle of authority and seed *breaks* the victim mentality. The victim mentality says, "I can't succeed until you allow me to succeed." When you take your authority and sow the kingdom into your life, the Bible says *"…thou shalt make thy way prosperous, and then thou shalt have good success"* (Joshua 1:8).

Sowing the kingdom and tending it faithfully means you study the Word, meditate on the Word, and do what the Word says, and then you make your way successful — you make your way prosperous. Jesus was teaching this more directly when He said:

*"If ye abide in me, and my words abide in you, ye
shall ask what ye will, and it shall be done unto you.
Herein is my Father glorified, that ye bear much fruit;
so shall ye be my disciples"* (John 15:7-8).

A man's harvest in life is based solely on the seeds he
has sown. So, all the principles you are learning here and
all the parables of the kingdom point to this fundamental
law: God's system is the law of seedtime and harvest.

The Bible declares in Genesis 8:22 that as long as the
earth remains, as long as there is cold and heat, day and
night, so there is seedtime and harvest.
This does not just apply to money
and it certainly doesn't just apply to
agriculture. It is God's entire system
of operation for all creation.

*The principle
of authority
and seed
breaks the
victim mentality.*

The Bible declares in Proverbs
18:24 that if you want a friend, you
have to be friendly. Jesus said if you
want His forgiveness, then you must
first forgive others (Matthew 6:14-
15). In fact, He said judgment will
come back to you in the same measure
you use to judge others (Matthew 7:1).

Galatians 6:1 says you who are spiritual are to restore
your brother lest you fall into the same temptation. You
see, God is teaching us that His system of operation is
seedtime and harvest. That which you sow, you will also
reap.

Nothing just happens in life. This is so hard for most people to digest. I know life is tough. I know it's hard to believe sometimes that God wants you blessed because life teaches you otherwise. People struggle in their minds. They do not want to take personal responsibility or get honest with themselves. Most people do not want to look at the seeds they have sown because they are not happy with the harvest in their lives. You must take a long, hard look at your life and realize you may not like the harvest, but you are responsible because of the seeds you have sown. Galatians 6:7 says:

> *"Be not deceived; God is not mocked: for whatsoever a man soweth, that shall he also reap."*

Again, I tell you—nothing just happens. There are spiritual laws that govern the natural realm. Remember Genesis 8:22: It says as long as the earth remains, so does seedtime and harvest. And until you recognize where you are, you will not be able to take the necessary steps to move ahead to the future.

A Responsibility to God's System

"Therefore I say unto you, Take no thought for your life, what ye shall eat, or what ye shall drink; nor yet for your body, what ye shall put on. Is not the life more than meat, and the body than raiment? Behold the fowls of the air: for they sow not, neither do they reap, nor gather into barns; yet your heavenly Father feedeth them. Are ye not much better than they?" (Matthew 6:25-26).

Verse 26 of this passage is crucial. What God is saying is the birds are not privileged to be part of God's system of doing things. They do not get to sow and they do not get to reap, and yet God takes care of them. How much more opportunity do you have because you have been given the promise of sowing and reaping?

Highlight this sentence with your pen: Your destiny is not in the hands of anyone else. When it comes to success or failure in life, your destiny is in your own hands because God has allowed you the privilege of being a part of His system.

> *"And he said, So is the kingdom of God, as if a man should cast seed into the ground... But when the fruit is brought forth, immediately he putteth in the sickle, because the harvest is come"* (Mark 4:26, 29).

Taking Action

I want you to do something to help you keep this teaching with you. Take a blank card or heavy paper and cut it to a size just small enough to fit into your pocket. On one side of the card, print this phrase:

God's system is the law of seedtime and harvest.

On the other side of the card, print these words:

Sow the Word of Promise — Expect a Harvest.

Carry this card around with you for at least 30 days. It will get in your way every time you reach into your pocket but that will be a way of tending the seedlings of these kingdom Truths that are hopefully being planted in the good soil of your heart.

This is God's system — seedtime and harvest. The emphasis is on *faith* but you have to understand how faith operates according to His system. Faith won't work for you if you neglect the system in which it operates.

Being Prepared

"For the earth bringeth forth fruit of herself; first the blade, then the ear, after that the full corn in the ear" (Mark 4:28).

Verse 28 is also very important. It demonstrates the progression or time involved in sowing and reaping. You do not just plant corn seed today and eat an ear of corn tomorrow. The progression (the system) must be followed. That is why you cannot wait until you are sick to follow the principles of seedtime and harvest. You cannot wait until you are broke. You cannot wait until you are down and out and then start planting seed and expect to reap immediate relief from your present pain. You must follow the principles of seedtime and harvest as a lifestyle.

Noah is a great example of a man who planned ahead and followed the seedtime and harvest principles. He built the ark *before* the storm arrived. There was no need for it beforehand but he prepared in advance. Likewise, you cannot wait until you are in a storm to start searching for scripture. You need to start building now.

Build by faith so you are instant in season and out of season. Noah's boat did not work until the storm came. All you've been sowing and building will arise for you when the storm comes into your life. When you put a demand on the Word, it will work. At the right time, the harvest will come forth. That is why the Bible declares the just must live by faith (Habakkuk 2:4).

Living by faith is a lifestyle. Faith is the motivating and organizing force of my life. Every day, moment-by-moment, I live by the Word of God. I do not just pick up the Word of God when I'm in a crisis. I experience a perpetual harvest in my life because I continually plant the seed—the Word of God—into my life.

"But seek ye first the kingdom of God, and his righteousness; and all these things shall be added unto you" (Matthew 6:33).

Seek first the kingdom of God. Seek first God's way of doing things. Seek first sowing a seed. Seek first seedtime and harvest. Seek first these things and all the other things will be added unto you.

Remember, the only thing you can expect to manifest is what you have sown in life.

Acting on Faith

"…If ye have faith as a grain of mustard seed, ye shall say unto this mountain, Remove hence to yonder place; and it shall remove…" (Matthew 17:20).

I want you to read and study Matthew 17:14-21. If you have the Word like a seed, nothing will be impossible for you. If you have the Word as a seed, then you can use that Word and speak to a mountain and it will move. Nothing shall be impossible.

Likewise, in Luke 17:5-6, the disciples ask for more faith. Jesus tells them if they have faith like the grain of mustard seed, they could say to the sycamine tree to be plucked up and be planted by the sea and it would obey them.

A mustard seed is one of the smallest seeds in existence. Jesus was telling the disciples the size of their faith was not the problem. The same is true for you. Getting more faith is not what you need when you do not exercise the faith you have properly. There is a system. You have to use the Word of God, operating in the system of seedtime and harvest, and it will produce God's promise in your life.

In Conclusion

Everything that operates within the kingdom of God is based upon the system of God—sowing and reaping. Jesus is called the firstborn among many brethren because He was the seed that fell to the ground and died. And at His resurrection, He was the Firstfruit of a great harvest. He is the Seed of God. God sowed His own Son in death and has reaped a great family of newborn, loving children. He then sowed His spirit of power into the firstfruits of the church (the disciples) and has continually reaped a massive army of warriors for the Truth.

God also sowed Abraham into the Promised Land and reaped a nation. He sowed the Law into the house of Israel and reaped its influence on all of history. We can find endless fulfillments of this system of sowing and reaping.

I believe God has promised you many great things. It is not just about your finances, although finances are included. It is about every area of your life. It is about your marriage, your children, your spiritual well-being, and your emotions. God says there is a system in operation for *all* these things.

You need to stop relying on the world's system and begin operating within the kingdom of God—His system, His methodology, His principle of seedtime and harvest.

My prayer is that you will begin to sow today and that you will have a glorious future of reaping tomorrow. My prayer is for you to stop working within the world's system and begin living by faith in God's system.

Live by the Word of God and you, too, will live in perpetual harvest.

Taking Action

Before we move on to the final part of this book, let's revisit the principles of taking possession of God's promises. Make several photocopies of page 86 and tape them every place you frequent to remind you of the lessons of seedtime and harvest. Post them on your bathroom mirror, by your computer monitor at work, on your refrigerator, and beside your bed so you can work on committing them to meditation before you go to sleep.

#1 Leave and Cleave

Leave your past behind you and cleave to tomorrow and what is promised you.

#2 Change Your Focus

Stop looking at your circumstances in front of you and lift up your eyes. Change your perspective and your attitude.

#3 Vision: See It and Receive It

You will die without vision. Be sensitive to the glimpse God gives you about the future He wants you to possess.

#4 Understand the Purpose for the Storm

When God gives you a revelation, the enemy will send a storm (a distraction) to take away the Word. God will use the storm to build your patience so you can inherit the promise.

#5 Endurance: It Takes Commitment

Make the decision to be consistent in your faith so that God will deliver His promise to you. You are only rewarded for that which you endure in life.

#6 Learn to Operate in God's System

There are two systems in operation—the world's system and God's system. If you operate in God's system, your needs will be met. To do that, you must seek first the kingdom of God, understand what the kingdom is, and operate in that kingdom.

#7 Seedtime and Harvest

You have a seed to plant and the authority to plant it, but remember: The seed you plant today is what you will reap tomorrow. So, don't wait until you're sick or broke to plant your seeds!

Part IV

Changing Your Perception of Prosperity

"But those things which proceed out of the mouth come forth from the heart…"

(Matthew 15:18)

Throughout this book, I stressed the fact that all the principles you've learned are not just about your money. This part of the book deals specifically with your money. Of course, as you read, I want you to keep in mind that the following principles can easily apply to all other areas of your life. But most people claim the majority of drama in their lives stems from money problems. So, I'm going to teach you some simple, yet powerful, truths about your money. I'm going to teach you how it isn't a *lack* of money causing the drama in your life. It's your *perception* of money that causes the drama in your life. Get your highlighter pen and notebook ready because you'll want to revisit this chapter many times in the future.

The Principles of Financial Positioning

Let's examine the principles of how you can position yourself financially. Before we begin, however, I want to say again that *wholeness* and *prosperity* are not just about money. But this section is focused on money, your perception of money, your attitude about money, your respect for money, and your future abundance, specifically about your finances.

Perspective Is Everything

Perspective is everything! Remember, in Genesis 13:14, God told Abram:

> *"Lift up now thine eyes, and look from the place where thou art…"*

He wanted Abram to change his perspective so he could see all God had promised him. If you can begin to see what God has promised you, then you can also begin to see your finances in a different light. Remember what you read earlier in this book? If you can see it, you can receive it! Poverty of any kind is a mindset, a mentality.

So, how can you begin to change your mindset when that painful memory is so rooted inside of your heart? I know, so many years have passed and you still can't seem to let go of that hurt. But it's easier than you think. Just pick up your Bible and make the Word work for you.

The answer is *forgiveness*. Remember the first Biblical reason for lack in your life (page 20-21)? Forgiveness releases you from bondage. Matthew 6:14-15 says:

> *"For if ye forgive men their trespasses, your heavenly Father will also forgive you: But if ye forgive not men their trespasses, neither will your Father forgive your trespasses."*

Surely, you don't expect God to bless you financially while you hold an unforgiving heart? Look at Romans 5:5:

> *"And hope maketh not ashamed; because the love of God is shed abroad in our hearts by the Holy Ghost which is given unto us."*

In other words, if *love* can be shed abroad in our hearts, so can forgiveness. You have to forgive all things intentionally and unintentionally done to you for your heart to be open and ready to receive God's blessing.

If you have a problem with your attitudes and perceptions of money, then we need to break that off of you and get to the root of the problem. That problem may be unforgiveness.

Define the Role of Money in Your Life

What do you want your money to do for you? Money without purpose is simply materialism. If you spend money on things that have no value to you, then you're just "buying stuff." But if you plan your purchases and value what you spend your money on, then that's an investment.

First Timothy 6:10 says, "For the love of money is the root of all evil…" It doesn't say *money* is the root of all evil. It says the *love of money* is the root of all evil. Money is simply a resource, a vehicle, a tool, a means to accomplishing what God wants you to do.

You know God has given you a calling in life and He will give you all the resources, including money, to accomplish it. But if you use that money in a way that dishonors Him or even in an honorable way that interferes with your calling, then He will not bless it. It's foolish to receive from God and not regard His will. You've heard it said that a fool and his money are soon parted, so you should examine your motives about money.

What Are Your Motives?

It is important to know your motives when it comes to money. You see, God wants you to be blessed. He wants money to be channeled through you for one, primary reason: So you can be a blessing to others.

Matthew 20:20 records an excellent example of what I mean by "motive." It says: "Then came to Him the mother of Zebedee's children with her sons, worshipping Him …"

In case you haven't read this Bible passage, I'll fill you in: This woman, Salome, was on a mission. But first, we see she was doing a good thing—*worshipping* Jesus. The word *worship* means "worth ship" and Jesus is certainly worthy of our worship, wouldn't you agree? But you can do a good thing for the wrong reason.

Reading further, we see she came, "desiring a certain thing of Him." Oh, she *desired a certain thing* from Jesus. She *wanted* something from Him. But that's not necessarily wrong, is it? Paul tells us to make our requests known to God (Philippians 4:6).

Let's look at what Salome wanted and see if we can understand her motives. Matthew 20:21 says, ". . . She saith unto him, Grant that these my two sons may sit, the one on thy right hand, and the other on the left, in thy kingdom."

Salome's husband was a wealthy fisherman. She was accustomed to having a better life than most women during that time. Her motive was that she wanted to make sure her sons were in a position to guarantee her current level of comfort. You see, when Jesus talked about His kingdom, most of His flock believed He was talking about an *earthly* kingdom, that He would be an *earthly* king with great wealth, and they, as His disciples, would also be rewarded with *earthly* treasures for their faith.

Salome was a follower of Jesus. She knew of His power and she probably knew of His lineage from David that qualified Him for the throne of Israel. She decided to approach Jesus, worshipfully but with an eye on gaining benefit for herself. This is a perfect example of doing the right thing but having the wrong motive.

Here's a question for you: Did you turn to this section of the book *first* hoping to find a magic shortcut to financial prosperity? If so, then the Bible says you have an evil eye because you are impatient about money (Proverbs 28:22). You're trying to go around God's entire counsel and skip to the part that might get you what you want.

You can't shortcut with God. Stop dancing with the devil with the blue dress on and let God have His way with your journey because He's going to have His way anyway, whether you like it or not.

Taking Action

Get a piece of paper and write down this question: "What are my motives concerning money?" Then, spend some time writing down the answers to that question. Is it just to give you power? Just to buy you things? Is it all about you, you, you? If you answer that question in a way that is not in alignment with what God wants for your money, then God will not bless you with your money. He will either withhold it from you or let it become a curse to you until you repent.

Your Past Holds the Key to Your Future

Ecclesiastes 1:9 says:

"The thing that hath been, it is that which shall be; and that which is done is that which shall be done…"

In other words, the root to financial freedom in your life is not an expensive financial planner, a big paycheck, an education, or a good banker.

The root is this: *It's all in your head!* It's in your memories. It's the way you learned to think and perceive. It's not in money itself, but in your perception of money that was formed in your past.

It's foolish to receive from God and not regard His will.

Now, go back to your childhood and think about how you first perceived money. How were you taught to feel about it? When you say or read the word "*money*" what comes to mind? What emotions do you feel? Anger? Resentment? Fear? Envy? Covetousness? Pride? Or do you feel nothing? Do you feel safety? Peacefulness? Gratitude? Cheerfulness in giving? Hope?

Identify the place where you first formed your perception of money. You can't conquer what you don't confront and you can't confront what you don't identify!

Here is a good illustration to make my point. I have a friend who told me about an experience he had when he was about 12 years old. His pastor, whom he respected very much, took him and some other boys to a restaurant. They all ordered shakes and burgers. Afterward, each of the boys put five dollars toward the bill. My friend said he didn't know he would need money and so he didn't have any. He was unable to contribute. Other boys in the group made fun of him for not paying his share. He was embarrassed and humiliated.

Today, that young man is an over-spender. He is in serious debt because he compulsively overspends. He picks up the tab at every meal because he needs to *prove*

If you don't respect money, it won't respect you.

he can. That terrible experience with money he suffered as a boy stayed with him into his adulthood and like shockwaves from an earthquake, he still feels the tremors in his life. He is a prisoner to that memory. God's promise to him about His finances is in bondage to that memory.

So, the question for you is: What was consciously and/or unconsciously taught to you about money? Did you learn to be careless with money? Or were you taught to respect money and take care of it?

You Attract What You Respect in Life

Regarding all things, you attract what you respect in life. If you don't respect money, it won't respect you. You have to *value* money. Money is attracted to people who respect it.

If you've shut the door on the six Biblical causes for a spirit of poverty (see page 18) and you're still struggling and not moving forward, then the problem is not likely a *lack* of money in your life. It's your way of thinking. If you have looked into your past and found you have a negative perspective of money, then the devil took advantage of your innocence as a child and lied to you.

There are words of power and words of destruction.

I want you to *know* the devil is a liar. But he's supposed to lie. He's the father of lies. But if I can change your perspective about this, then you can begin to see what God has promised you.

Once again, what you don't respect, you won't attract in life. That applies to money, anointing, your gifts, relationships, the Spirit of God, your husband, your wife, or anything else that has value. So among other things, get your money in order.

Order is the respectful arrangement of things. If you don't have order in your life, then you'll have no authority to move forward in your life.

Acknowledge That Words Have Power

Did you know you can lie to yourself about your life situation and your life will believe it? It's true! James 1:22 says:

> *"But be ye doers of the word, and not hearers only, deceiving your own selves."*

Yes, you can deceive yourself into thinking you have poverty and you will have poverty. Matthew 15:18 says:

Taking Action

Here's an interesting exercise: Take out your wallet or your purse and open it. Go to where you hold your money, checkbook, and credit cards.

Now, open your checkbook and observe the ledger. Does it contain the proper dates? The check numbers? To whom you wrote the check? An amount and a balance adjusted?

Now look at your cash. Is it all wadded up? Are the bills out of order and your change jumbling around in your pocket?

What about your credit cards? Are they shoved into your wallet in no particular order? Do you have three or four expired cards you can't use anymore?

If you answered "yes" to any of these questions, then

"But those things which proceed out of the mouth come forth from the heart; and they defile the man."

Just because your mouth says it makes it true? Yes, because it comes from the heart and that's a poor excuse to stay in poverty!

There are words of power and words of destruction. Your words create your world. Matthew 12:37 says:

"For by thy words thou shalt be justified, and by thy words thou shalt be condemned."

you don't respect your money. A man who respects his money will often have a money clip even if he only has three $1 bills. If a man can respect $3, then God can trust him with $3,000. And if he can respect $3,000, then God can trust him with $3 million.

Do yourself a favor: Buy a good wallet or pocketbook. Get rid of the old, outdated credit cards and clean out the old receipts. Arrange your cash in the proper order and make sure your checkbook is always neatly up to date. Also, make sure your checks have stubs or duplicate copies. It will help you keep better track of your expenses. These things are not only valuable habits that will keep you better organized but they will help change your perspective about money. If you *act* respectfully toward your money, you'll *become* respectful toward money.

But look at what Ephesians 3:20 says:

"Now unto him that is able to do exceeding abundantly above all that we ask or think, according to the power that worketh in us."

This Scripture is telling us the *power worketh in us*. Remember what I taught you earlier about God giving you power to get wealth. That power is *in* us.

If your child goes shopping with you and asks for something, don't say, "We can't afford that." When you speak those words, you are speaking life into that statement and planting a seed into your child that will bear fruit when he or she becomes an overspender someday. Also, that statement surrenders your authority over your money. That's not respect, that's worship. Money is a tool, not a governor over you.

Instead, look at your child and ask, "How can we afford that?" By taking the matter in that direction, you are helping your child develop his or her own problem-solving skills. You are helping your child think about the value of things. You are showing respect for money by being accountable to your budget. And you are preserving your authority over your money by looking for a way to use it wisely.

So, stop the negative power of the "can't" word over your money. You may not always find a way to afford something immediately, but you can maintain the right perspective about your money and work a plan to make the purchase later. Proverbs 6:2 says:

"Thou art snared with the words of thy mouth,
thou art taken with the words of thy mouth."

That means start eliminating words and phrases like "I can't" and "I don't know how" and "I am unable" from your vocabulary. By your words, you hinder or unleash God's power in you. Start saying "I can" and "I will" and "I am learning" and "All things are possible" and see how God moves in your life. Look at Proverbs 5:2. It says:

"That thou mayest regard discretion, and
that thy lips may keep knowledge."

And Numbers 14:28 says:

"Say unto them, As truly as I live, saith the LORD, as
ye have spoken in mine ears, so will I do to you…"

God *does* what you *speak.* Proverbs 21:23 says:

"Whoso keepeth his mouth and his tongue
keepeth his soul from troubles."

In other words, tell yourself to "shut up" sometimes! Before you speak, ask yourself, "Are my words in alignment with God's will?" Unfortunately, we are all guilty of negative speaking and thinking at one time or another. Find an accountability partner and let other people help you to stop speaking destruction into your life through your words.

Value Your Position in Christ

You can only overcome your condition by your position in Christ Jesus. Until you recognize who you are—a joint heir with Christ (that means everything that is His is also yours)—no one will place value on your efforts. It's one thing to be poor, but it's another thing to *feel* poor. Deuteronomy 8:18 says:

> *"But thou shalt remember the LORD thy God: for it is he that giveth thee power to get wealth, that he may establish his covenant which he sware unto thy fathers, as it is this day."*

In other words, your name is on it, so you can be certain. Here are some practical tips for holding up your value to the world:

- When you go to buy something (like a car) let them offer a price first. Then you negotiate. Hold your head up, speak clearly, and know the power of God is working in you. Don't be afraid! Second Timothy 1:7 says, *"For God hath not given us the spirit of fear; but of power, and of love, and of a sound mind."* This is not about "self" or how much power you have. This is about God's power in you. It's not about how you see yourself. It's about how God sees you. You are a sanctuary, a house of God. James 1:5-6 says:

> *"If any of you lack wisdom, let him ask of God, that giveth to all men liberally, and upbraideth not; and it shall be given him. But let him ask in faith, nothing wavering. For he that wavereth is like a wave of the sea driven with the wind and tossed."*

- Before you begin a phone call, go into a business meeting, or start negotiations on a house or a car, seek God's power and wisdom over your decisions. Pray to Him for wisdom. He will speak through you. He will communicate the verbal and non-verbal signals to those with whom you are dealing and they will value your words and actions. They will respect you, even if they don't understand *why* they respect you. So, value yourself. Be convinced of how God sees you.

- There is one other thing that communicates how you value yourself. The way you dress says a lot to others about your personal value. Make sure your clothes are clean and pressed. They don't have to be expensive. I have found great looking suits at Goodwill! Make sure your hands and nails are cleaned and trimmed and your hair is styled and neat. You don't have to spend hours on your appearance to look self-respecting. If you have to spend that much time, you'll just look like someone who's insecure and needs to project a false impression. But people do *see* you before they *hear* you. So, always be ready to make a good first impression.

Learn to Make Your Money Work for You

There are three ways to become financially well-provided for:

1. Work hard all your life.

2. Receive a gift, an inheritance, or win the lottery.

3. Make good investments.

Number one is the simple and lifelong way to make money—and it is a noble way. Paul says, in 1 Thessalonians 4:11:

> *"…to be quiet, and to do your own business, and to work with your own hands…"*

So, it's good to work hard. Your grandparents would say it's the honest way to live your life. Toil and drudgery need not be the lifelong occupation of anyone, but honest, meaningful work is holy and will even be part of our lives in heaven.

You shouldn't count on Number Two, even if you have a rich relative or consider yourself the luckiest person on earth. Counting on these things could be an invitation to laziness and irresponsibility. Inheritance is a blessing though! Build on the foundation that was left to you.

As for Number Three, the key to accelerating your earnings is to make your money work for you. You must begin to think of every dime you spend as an investment. If you can't see the investment value in something you are about to buy, you're probably robbing from your financial prosperity.

Deuteronomy 15:6 says:

> *"…thou shalt lend unto many nations, but thou shalt not borrow…"*

That means you have to learn to sacrifice *now* for what you want in the future. Think about that dress you can't live without. Is it worth it to go into debt for that $100 dress? Well, that $100 dress you bought on your credit card will be old in two weeks and you could wind up paying over $200 for it by the time you pay off the credit card bill.

Did you know the average American family has $8,000 in credit card debt? Let me tell you something—if you make the minimum payments, it will take you a *lifetime* to pay off $8,000 in credit card debt. Credit card companies don't want you to pay off your debt. Your debt is what earns them money and they earn it off your future prosperity. The same goes for those rent to own businesses. They get rich off your minimum payments and you spend a lifetime keeping them in the lap of luxury.

It will take you a lifetime to pay off $8,000 in credit card debt.

There's a better more godly way to provide for yourself. Tithe faithfully, save some, pay cash (as opposed to credit) for your purchases, and invest the interest you aren't paying to someone else. Pay that interest to yourself. Open a savings account, at the very least. Learn about investment accounts available at your bank. Find out when and if your bank holds investing seminars. Consider joining an investing club—you can find them in every city.

Investing wisely over a long period of time with God's blessing is the best and strongest way to build financial prosperity. Here's an example: If you are 18 and you save $100 a month in an IRA, by the time you retire at 65 you will have close to a million dollars. That's right! That's only $25 a week. That's only $3.75 a day! You can spend more than that on coffee! But saving $1,200 a year, even at an average interest rate, will prove to be the smartest investment you ever made. So, invest wisely and consistently.

Character Is Character

This is so important, I'll have you read it again and highlight it…Character is character.

You would be wise not to go into business with a person who does not tithe. A non-tither robs from God. And if he steals from God, he will surely steal from you. Don't join hands in business with someone who doesn't acknowledge God as the Lord of his profit (fruit).

You must ask the right questions about people with whom you do business. Look at their obligations, their education, and their personal life. Don't get caught in a situation where you get ripped off and all you can say is, "I didn't know." Learn how they handle money, how they manage their money. Ask about their budget. Ask about their investments. Ask about their balance sheet and learn how to read a financial statement.

Psalm 24:4, 5 says:

> *"He that hath clean hands, and a pure heart…*
> *shall receive the blessing from the Lord."*

Always make sure any person with whom you align yourself has clean hands and a pure heart. This is important because what you don't know can curse you. Don't make a covenant with a person who doesn't understand that character is character. Don't let them near your stuff if they don't take care of their stuff. And this applies to your business, your finances, your emotions, and even your family.

In Conclusion

In this section we have focused specifically on money. But the truths you have learned in these pages should apply to every area of your life. You can simply replace every word in this section that referred to money with other words like giftings, talents, time, and relationships.

In all these areas, you must *identify* the areas of your life that need revelation and healing. How do you feel about yourself? Your money? Your time? Your gifts? Your relationships? Do you have shame, fear, envy, or covetousness in your heart?

Remember this: You can't conquer what you don't confront. And you can't confront what you don't identify.

Final Words from Pastor Paula

Everything you've read in this book encompasses a theme based on one passage in Scripture—Deuteronomy 8:18.

"But thou shalt remember the LORD thy God: for it is he that giveth thee power to get wealth, that he may establish his covenant which he sware unto thy fathers, as it is this day."

I urge you to memorize this passage because it will serve you in many areas of your life. It will help you remember that you have *power* to reap and *authority* to sow your seed. It will help you remember the Source of that power and authority. And when you speak these words, you will be speaking Truth into your life.

Remember, anything which you expect God to bless and be Lord of is represented in some way by a firstfruit. That irrevocable firstfruit belongs to God and God alone. First things are set apart for God and touching them for personal gain or use brings a curse on the firstfruit and everything with which the firstfruit gets mixed. It is the law. Firstfruit your increase and all your increase thereafter will be blessed.

If you have heard my preachings on these subjects, then you know how passionate I am about them. It's because I am mad! I am mad at that spirit deceiving you and blinding you. I am mad at that spirit keeping you out of the fullness of God's plan, and destroying your mind and your money. I'm tired of you being harassed by the devil. I'm tired of your marriages breaking up and your children being on drugs. I'm tired of you being broke and the devil getting the best of you. I know the lack in your life isn't because of a lack of love for God. It's because the enemy keeps you blinded and ignorant and what you don't know can wreck your life. So, I'm mad at the devil. In fact, I'm mad as hell at the devil! But I say "No more!" God's people are getting a breakthrough!

God is looking for Christians to become a people whose God is the Maker of their city, a people who put Him first, who stand firm and see the salvation of the Lord. You cannot violate God's principles and plead promises expecting Him to bless your mess. You have to get things in order.

As you continue your journey, may the Lord bless you with His promise. But may He guide you to a place of healing and wholeness first so you can truly be in a place to experience possession of your promise.

Praise the Lord!

If you don't know Jesus Christ as your personal Lord and Savior, you are encouraged to make this decision today as you pray the following prayer:

Heavenly Father, I recognize and admit that I am a sinner. I turn from my sins, confess with my mouth, and believe in my heart that Jesus is Lord. I believe that He lived, died, and was raised from the dead for my salvation. I receive my salvation and all of its benefits right now. Lord, thank You for saving me this day. In Jesus' name, I pray. Amen!

To learn more about Paula White Ministries and Without Walls International Church, please write to:

Paula White Ministries
Media Ministry of Without Walls
International Church
PO Box 25151
Tampa FL 33622
813-873-2441

Or call the Prayer Line at 813-874-7729

Visit the website at www.paulawhite.org

Product order line: 800-992-8892

Notes

Notes

Notes